V is for VETERAN

ISBN: 978-1-7348227-6-2 (hardcover)
ISBN: 978-1-7348227-7-9 (softcover)
ISBN: 978-1-7348227-8-6 (ebook)

10 9 8 7 6 5 4 3 2 1

First Edition

ACKNOWLEDGEMENTS

Dancey Creel

Clifford Coke Hopping, Korean War Veteran, U.S. Navy, HM2 - Hospital Corpsman Second Class (1933-2017)

Papa - Strong and steady, peaceful and patient, calm and caring, with grit and grace - thank you for your example. You were light in the darkness and you loved me best. My hero, you are.

Cleatus Lebow, World War II Veteran, US Navy, USS Indianapolis, FT3 - Fire Control Technician, Petty Officer Third Class (1924-)

Cleatus - My friend, I honor you, today and every day. Thank you for your service, sacrifice, and strength; thank you for 20 years of letters and friendship. Knowing you, is a highlight of my life.

Coke Hopping

Dad - Thank you for planting, deep in my soul, this faith in God, this love for country, and this yearning for peace. Poised in my eye is this tear to be shed when the National Anthem sounds and the American flag proudly flies - all because of you. I miss you. Strength and Honor.

Edie Hopping Coker

Mom - Thank you for sharing your love of literature, your way with words, and mostly for your earnest encouragement for all I do. I love you.

Chet Creel

Chet – Thank you for telling pink-puppy dog stories, remixing "Hush, Little Baby," and for reading countless bed-time books to our babies. We are grateful you are ours.

Kyle & Greg

Gents - Thank you for this "yes."

CW4 (R) Gregory Coker

MSG Leon Hanson, GWOT (Global War on Terrorism) Veteran - Delta Force Commando, B Squadron

It was an honor to serve with him protecting our great country and making history together. Our friendship and his name will never be forgotten. RIP brother, I love you. **Rangers Lead the Way!**

MSG George E. Hand IV, Mogadishu and GWOT (Global War on Terrorism) Veteran – Delta Force Commando, A Squadron

George is my good friend, and he inspired, encouraged and contributed in the writing of my stories. George is truly an amazing man and a great American.

SGM Kyle E. Lamb, Mogadishu and GWOT (Global War on Terrorism) Veteran - Delta Force Commando, C Squadron

Our friendship is very valuable to me. Kyle's faith and inspiration helped lead me to write my stories so others may understand. It was an honor to serve with him in combat. **Stay in the Fight!**

Edie E. Coker

Thank you for your love, inspiration, and trust in God; you are an amazing woman. I love you!

True and Haven Creel

These two granddaughters make my heart sing every day, and I love them to the moon and back.

Wyatt and Whitney Price

My original dreams of being a grandfather and a blessing from God. I love them more than they know.

These few people are very important in my life and a great representation of why I was willing to lay down my life to protect our country, our rights as Americans, and our freedom.
It was my honor and a true privilege to be a special operations soldier.

Kyle Wagner

Bill H. Wagner, Korean War Veteran

Grandad - Thank you for the many stories you've told me over the years of your time in the Navy. It's these little reminders of service to your country that helped inspire me to help create this book. I love you.

Jimmie C. Johnson II, Operation Enduring Freedom Veteran

Jim - Thank you for your heroic service over your many tours.

To the many family and friends that have all served honorably in the Armed Forces:

Grandad, Granddaddy Shannon, Grandpa Jerry, Big Jim, Uncle Jim, Jason Wooldridge, Greg Coker, Ryan Baker, Travis Gerdes, Cody Spurgeon, Trent Layman, and the countless others I'm sure I have missed - THANK YOU

ARMED FORCES

The **armed forces** - or **military** - of the
United States of America
is made up of **six branches**:

Army, Navy, Marine Corps,
Air Force, Space Force, and Coast Guard.

BRAVERY

Soldiers are known for their bravery.

It doesn't mean they are fearless. Instead, it means they do something even though it may be scary. They may not know what will happen next, but the soldiers in the picture are bravely continuing their mission.

Their bravery and courage keeps us safe.

Constitution

The **Constitution** is the highest law, or set of rules, in the United States of America, and it belongs to all Americans! It creates our government and lists our rights as Americans. It was written in 1787, and for over 200 years, soldiers enlisted in the military have sworn to

"...support and defend the Constitution of the United States against all enemies, foreign and domestic..."

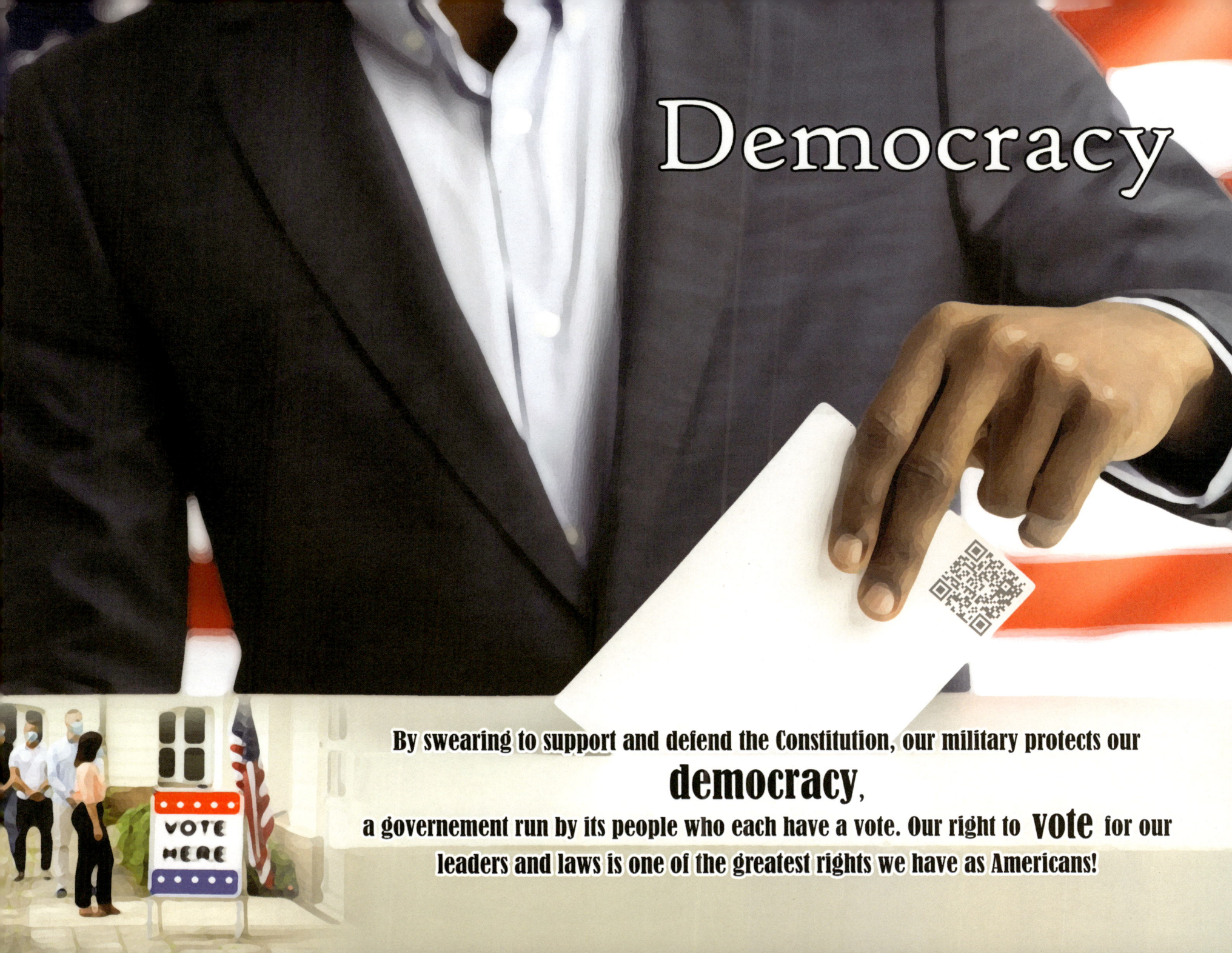

Democracy

By swearing to support and defend the Constitution, our military protects our
democracy,
a governement run by its people who each have a vote. Our right to **vote** for our
leaders and laws is one of the greatest rights we have as Americans!

E **IS FOR** **EQUALITY**

Equality is an American right that our military helps protect.

Equality means people are treated the same no matter who they are, what they look like, or where they're from.

I HAVE A DREAM

Many heroic people, such as Susan B. Anthony and Dr. Martin Luther King, inspired others to push for more equality for all Americans.

Everyone deserves equal opportunities in our country!

Family

Whether a *U.S. service member* is home or deployed, **family** plays an important role in their life. A strong **family**, **community**, and **self** are as important to the success of a service member as training.

On **September 11, 2001**,
also known as *9/11*,
the United States of America was
attacked. These attacks happened from New
York City to Washington, D.C., and many
people were hurt or died. The location of
the attack on the **World Trade Center**
in New York City is now known as
Ground Zero.

Ground Zero

Hero

Heroes are people who take action to make things better because it is the right thing to do.

Brave citizens from all walks of life, including *first responders* and *military personnel,* risked their lives to save and protect others on 9/11.

They are **heroes**.

I is for
INDEPENDENCE

J is for
JULY 4TH

When the **Founding Fathers** adopted the
Declaration of Independence
on **July 4, 1776**,
the United States of America separated from Britain
and became its own country.

 **K** is for **K.I.A. (Killed in Action)**

Service members put their lives at risk to protect us. Since the United States of America was formed, over 650,000 Americans have died in battle - or were **Killed in Action.**

LIBERTY

means that we get to decide many things about our lives -

what we do, where we go, what we say, what we eat -

as long as it doesn't put life at risk or take away another person's freedom.

Life, liberty, and the pursuit of happiness

are all rights our service members help protect.

MEMORIAL DAY

A *memorial* is something made to remind people of and celebrate a person or event.

Memorial Day is observed every year on the 4th Monday of May to remember service members who have died serving their country.

One of the most famous memorials in the United States is the Tomb of the Unknown Soldier at Arlington National Cemetary in Arlington, Virginia.

Wreaths have been laid at the tomb in a tradition that started in 1921.

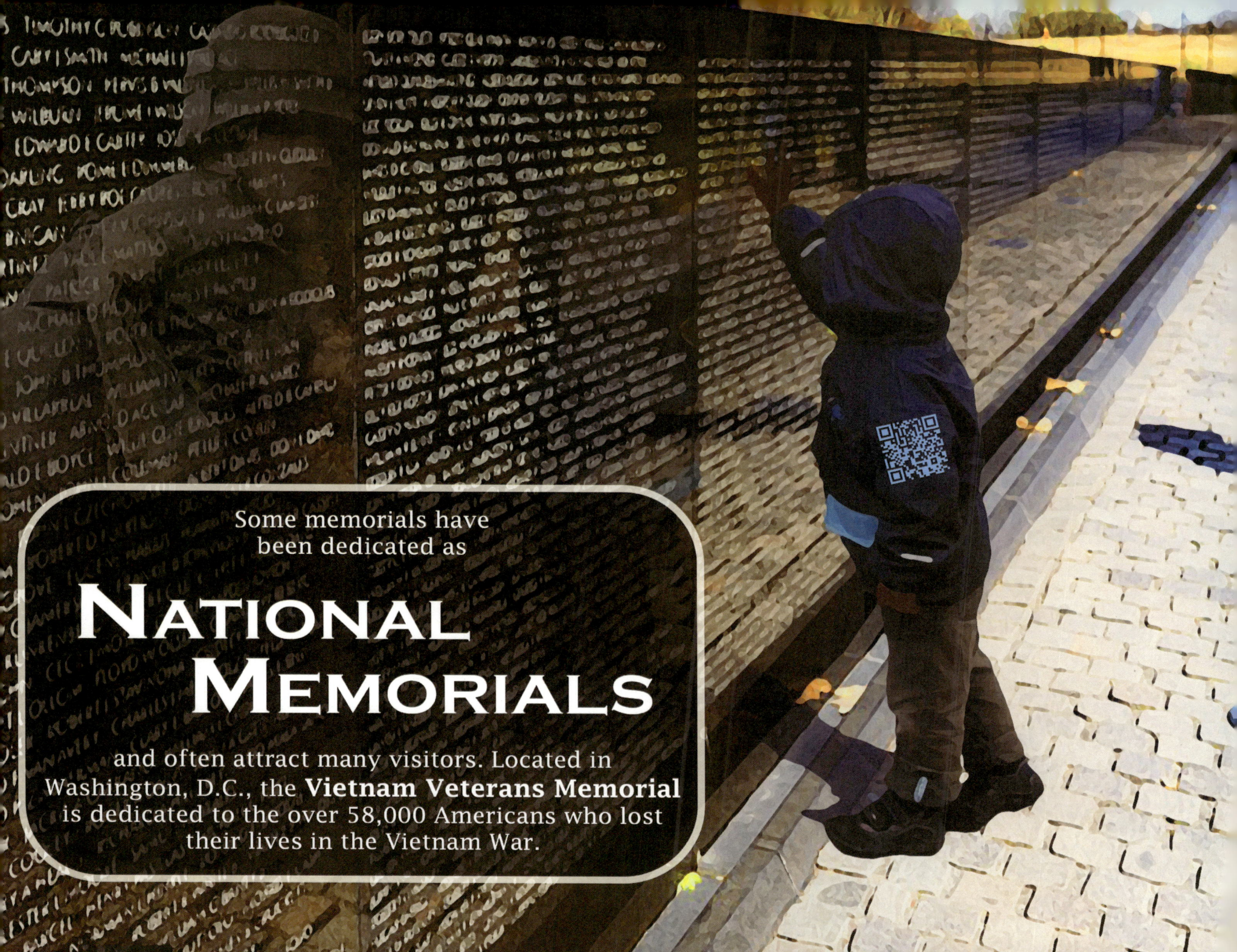

Some memorials have
been dedicated as

NATIONAL
MEMORIALS

and often attract many visitors. Located in
Washington, D.C., the **Vietnam Veterans Memorial**
is dedicated to the over 58,000 Americans who lost
their lives in the Vietnam War.

OLD GLORY

As Americans, we honor a flag that goes by many different names -
the Red, White, and Blue; the Stars and Stripes;
Old Glory ; the Star Spangled Banner -
and is one of the most recognizable flags in the world.

PLEDGE OF ALLEGIANCE

By saying the Pledge of Allegiance, we are
making a promise to be true to and protect
each other, our country, and our flag.

Quiet Professionals

Special Forces members, nicknamed

Quiet Professionals,

are trained to perform risky missions,
like sneaking into difficult places in a helicopter at night!

They often can speak several languages and
carry 100 pounds of gear in their rucksacks!

RESPECT AND REMEMBER

Americans of all ages, races, and backgrounds have a chance to chase their dreams due to the service members who protect our rights and freedoms.

It is important that, no matter what, we *respect* the service members and veterans who are with us today and *remember* those who are not.

SALUTE

One of the many ways that service members and veterans show respect to each other is to **salute**.
Though it is tradition and courtesy, it is more importantly a sign of *honor*, *recognition*, and *deference*.

The military protects American interests and those of our allies - or friends. American

TROOPS

are stationed all over the world!

Out of 1.35 million American service members, almost 1.2 million are stationed in our country - the **United States of America**.

A VETERAN

- whether active duty, discharged, retired, or reserve -
is someone who, at one point in his or her life, wrote a
blank check made payable to the United States of America
for an amount of "up to and including his or her life."

-Unknown

Honor to the soldier and sailor everywhere, who bravely bears his country's cause. Honor, also, to the citizen who cares for his brother in the field and serves, as he best can, the same cause.

-Abraham Lincoln

Sometimes, service members are seriously injured in combat. These

WOUNDED WARRIORS

carry the scars of their injuries long after the battle is over.

They are heroes.

...One Two Sierra **X-Ray** Hotel...

Service members use the **phonetic alphabet** to communicate letters or spelling without any mistakes. For every letter of the alphabet, a distinct word is used that starts with that letter. For example, the letter "X" in the english alphabet is "X-Ray" in the miltary phonetic alphabet!

We sleep safely in our beds because

brave men and women

go into the night to protect us -

Yesterday,

today,

and tomorrow.

Dancey Creel

Dancey's values, established in childhood, have proven the foundation on which she lives her life. She believes in kindness and loyalty, goodness and trust, improving situations when possible, and leaving people and places better than she finds them. Education and faith are vital and guide her direction and decisions. It is important to Dancey that her children understand and appreciate the privileges and responsibilities of living in these great United States. Every opportunity that presents itself can be a teachable moment, and Dancey is dedicated to recognizing those moments for her two daughters, True (8) and Haven (5). Dancey and her husband, Chet, are raising their family in an agricultural environment in Texas where they raise cattle, operate grain elevators, contribute to their community, and enjoy a blessed life.

 # CW4 (R) Gregory Coker US Army

CW4 (R) Gregory Coker served 22 years in the U.S. Army. After being specially recruited, assessed, and selected, he spent 15 years as an AH-6 "Little Bird" attack helicopter instructor pilot in the Army's only Special Operations Helicopter unit, the 160th Special Operations Aviation Regiment. He was one of the senior Lead Instructor Pilots responsible for planning and executing special operations missions in support of our nation's most elite special operations units. He achieved 7,400 hours of accident-free flying, over 6,200 hours of night vision goggles, and 1,500 hours of combat time. Additionaly, Coker supervised and directed teams of up to 300 soldiers in the planning and execution of numerous complex combat operations at the Joint Task Force level. He was responsible for leading and planning scores of real world combat missions with significant tactical, operational, and strategic value during Operation Enduring Freedom and Iraqi Freedom with 100% success in support of the Global War on Terrorism (GWOT) during his 11 combat tours from 2001-2008.

"Gravy" and his wife Edie, live in Graham and are very active in the community. He is a recently-published author and owns *Shield 91*, where he provides all aspects of firearms training, leadership development, executive team building, emergency response operations, security assessments, tactical planning, and helicopter operations. He developed a school safety and security program - *"Not on My Watch"* - that has been implemented in Texas and other states.

Kyle Wagner

Raised in Uvalde, TX, Kyle grew up listening to many stories of the past service of his grandfather and great-grandfathers. His great-grandfather was one of the last horseback cavalry to be stationed at Fort Clark in Brackettville, TX. An accomplished children's book author and illustrator, he started *Punkindooger Publishing* to provide literature to children that focuses on important people, events, and industries in our world, including the honorable service members and veterans that have served our country proudly. He also made giving back a core value at Punkindooger, and as part of its *Give to Grow* mission, a portion of the proceeds of every single item sold through Punkindooger benefits a related charitable organization. He, his wife Cye, daughter Davis, and son Conrad live in Fort Worth, TX and are proud to actively serve their community, state, and country through many organizations.

Punkindooger Publishing is a proud supporter of **Special Operations Warrior Foundation**. As part of its **Give to Grow** mission, Punkindooger is donating 10% of the proceeds of "V is for Veteran" to the Foundation, starting with a $5,000 commitment. Special Operations Warrior Foundation is a top-rated nonprofit organization that ensures full financial assistance for a post-secondary degree from an accredited two- or four-year college, university, technical, or trade school; and offers family and educational counseling, including in-home tutoring, to the surviving children of Army, Navy, Air Force, and Marine Corps special operations personnel who lose their lives in the line of duty. Special Operations Warrior Foundation also provides immediate financial assistance to severely wounded and hospitalized special operations personnel. For more information on Special Operations Warrior Foundation, please visit

www.specialops.org.

Lightning Source UK Ltd.
Milton Keynes UK
UKRC021626200521
383861UK00001BC/7